Celebrating the Gift of Marriage

James W. Moore

Celebrating the Gift of Marriage

DIMENSIONS
FOR LIVING

NASHVILLE

CELEBRATING THE GIFT OF MARRIAGE

Copyright © 2008 by Dimensions for Living

This book is printed on acid-free paper.

Library of Congress Cataloging-in-Publication Data

Moore, James W. (James Wendell), 1938–
 Celebrating the gift of marriage / James W. Moore
  p. cm.
 ISBN-13: 978-0-687-64701-9 (pbk. : alk. paper)
1. Marriage—Religious aspects—Methodist Church. 2. Methodist Church—Doctrines. I. Title.
 BX8349.M35M66 2008
 248.8'44—dc22

2007050553

Chapter 3 was previously printed as chapter 14, "Marriage and God— 'Celebrating the Gift of Marriage,'" in James W. Moore, *There's a Hole in Your Soul That Only God Can Fill* (Nashville: Dimensions for Living, 2005).

08 09 10 11 12 13 14 15 16 17—10 9 8 7 6 5 4 3 2 1

MANUFACTURED IN THE UNITED STATES OF AMERICA

For June

CONTENTS

FOREWORD
  by June D. Moore ix

Chapter 1
The Four C's of a Great Marriage 1

Chapter 2
In Real Estate, It's Location;
In Marriage, It's Communication. 13

Chapter 3
Celebrating the Gift of Marriage 27

Chapter 4
Happy Marriage: It's All about Choices 39

Chapter 5
The Church in Your House 51

Chapter 6
The Subtle Difference. 65

DISCUSSION/REFLECTION GUIDE
  by Sally D. Sharpe 73

FOREWORD

When I was invited to write the foreword for *Celebrating the Gift of Marriage*, I was honored and quite excited. You see, for years I have watched my husband write and create, and I have noticed the pleasure he gets from writing, as well as the deep satisfaction he feels in completing the task, knowing that with the help of God's guidance and God's grace, he has done his very best.

Celebrating the Gift of Marriage was written for engaged couples and for married couples who want to enrich their relationship, as well as for couples who may be struggling in their marriage. The pages of this book are filled with encouraging words based on the teachings of Jesus, helpful hints, and good advice, all with Jim's very special sense of humor.

I feel most fortunate and grateful for the wonderful and *fun* forty-eight years we have shared together in our marriage, which has been enriched over and over by the insights reflected in this book. It is my prayer that God will bless you and yours, as you celebrate the special gift of marriage!

—*June D. Moore*

1
The Four C's of a Great Marriage

KEY FOCUS: If you want to have a fulfilling marital relationship, you need communication, courtship, commitment, and Christ.

Read 1 Corinthians 13:1-7.

Why are we having so much trouble in our homes today? Why are so many marriages failing? One of the sad and painful commentaries on our modern-day world is the breakdown of family life and the breakup of so many marriages. Why is this happening, and what can we do about it?

Well, we need to understand that for a marriage to succeed and be happy and productive and fulfilling, four key things need to be happening in that relationship, what we might refer to as the four C's of a great marriage. Here they are.

The First "C" of a Great Marriage Is *Communication*

In a marriage, communication needs to be happening creatively on four levels: physical, social, intellectual, and spiritual. Those sound pretty obvious, but let's walk through these.

Physical communication is the communication of "touching," touching in all of the ways that married couples want and need to touch each other—sitting close to each other, hugging each other, kissing each other, holding each other, making love with each other. Physical communication, the communication of touching, is so important to a marriage. It's not sordid or ugly. It's a sacred and beautiful gift from God, not just for the procreation of children (as miraculous and as wonderful as that is), but also for the communication and celebration of our love for each other. When you fall in love with someone, you want to be close to that person, *physically* close to that person.

Now, I have read in books and magazines about platonic relationships in marriage—people who get married and just love each other's minds and never touch each other. Maybe that does happen, but I think it is very rare. Most people want and need to be touched. Most people want and need physical affection. Most people want and need physical intimacy.

And over the years I have noticed something: when communication breaks down in a marriage, most often the first place it raises a "red flag" is right here, in the area of physical intimacy. Let me show you what I mean with one type of example.

A young married couple goes to a crowded party, and all is beautiful. The husband is paying a lot of attention to his wife, and they are holding hands. They are being really sweet to each other. But then some of the husband's buddies from work show up, and that "macho thing" that sometimes gets into men rears its head, and the husband begins to show off for his buddies by teasing his wife. It starts out in good fun, but he gets carried away and takes it too far, and he embarrasses her. She becomes upset, and at that moment she wants to be physically away from him, so she turns and runs out of the room. The husband thinks, *Oh, no! Why do I do that?* He is remorseful and sorry, and he runs after her to apologize. He catches up with her in the crowded living room. He touches her arm, and what does she do? She pulls away! She does not want to be touched, because communication has broken down.

Now, on the other hand, when communication is right in our marriage, we want to be touched, and we want to touch back. Physical affection is so important. Now, let me hurry to say that I am not so Freudian that I think it's the only thing that matters

3

in a marriage, but I want to tell you that I have been around long enough to know that it's really important; it's *really* important!

Next is *social communication*. Social communication means being friends as well as lovers. It means being *best friends*. It means just enjoying life with each other; going for a walk together; going shopping together; watching TV together; taking in a movie together; sharing meals together; talking to each other; visiting with each other; being vulnerable with each other; knowing that this person, this mate, is going to love you even though you are not perfect. It means sharing together your hopes and your dreams, your victories and your defeats, your strengths and your weaknesses, your secrets and your fears, your joys and your sorrows.

Now, let me give you what I call "the Friendship Test." Imagine that you get a call this afternoon telling you that a distant relative in a distant city, a relative whom you didn't even know existed, had left you $30 million, tax free; who would be the first person or persons you would want to share that good news with? According to "the Friendship Test," that tells you who your friends are.

Or turn the coin over and imagine that instead of that call this afternoon, someone called to tell you that a person you love deeply had just been killed in a car wreck. Who would be the first person or persons you would want to share that bad news with? That also tells you who your friends are.

In a good marriage, in both of those instances, the first person to come to your mind would be your mate, because your marriage mate should be not only your lover but also your best friend, with whom you share the joys and sorrows of life. If the person you are married to is your best friend, then you have heaven on earth.

Look now at *intellectual communication*. Intellectual communication is sharing the world of ideas. What matters to you? What's important to you? What is your philosophy of life? What are your priorities? What are the things that make you who you are? To talk about those things and to share your values is so important. You don't have to think exactly alike. You don't have to agree on every single thing. You don't have to belong to the same political party. But what you *do* have to have is respect for your mate's point of view. You don't have to have the exact same philosophy of life, but to have the same virtues, the same ethics, and the same morality is so crucial.

I once saw a marriage come apart at the seams because the two people involved could not respect each other's approach to life. The wife was very compassionate and tenderhearted, especially toward persons in need in our society. She had grown up in a home where, when there was a problem in the city, her parents were the first ones there to help out—and that was part of who she was, a big part of her basic makeup.

But her husband was just the opposite. He accused her of interfering in other people's lives. He didn't want to help anybody, and especially not those different from him; and that intellectual, philosophical difference tore their marriage apart. It's so important to be able to communicate physically, socially, and intellectually.

Then there is *spiritual communication*. Spiritual communication is so important—to share God; to share the Scriptures; to share the church; to share the faith; to share at least a part of your prayer life is so important.

Now, let me tell you something that is fascinating here. Normally I read *Sports Illustrated*, but somebody once gave me a *Redbook* magazine that had an interesting article about love and marriage. *Redbook* had done a survey of several hundred couples, in which they had compared couples on two levels of communication—the spiritual and the physical. And *Redbook* magazine was honest enough to admit that they were surprised by their findings. They went into the survey expecting that those who had a strong spiritual grounding would not be very affectionate physically, and that those who were highly physically affectionate would not be very spiritual.

But do you know what they found out? It was exactly the opposite! Couples who were strongly spiritually close had a better physical relationship. Now, if you think about that closely, it makes a lot of sense. If you don't have a strong spiritual base, then physically you tend to see the other person as an object for your gratification. But if you are spiritually grounded, then you see the other person as a child of God, a person you love so much that you want to bring pleasure to her or him. And if you have two people thinking like that at the same time, you have something special indeed.

Think about it: what does it take to make someone a good love-mate? Well, it takes love and respect and tenderness and compassion and thoughtfulness, and that's what the spiritual life teaches us to be. The people in the survey who had a strong spiritual life, a healthy love for God, a healthy love for the church, a healthy love for other people, and a healthy self-esteem—those wonderfully spiritual people had a better love life. That finding surprised *Redbook* magazine, but it shouldn't surprise us because in the church we believe that the best sign of Christian discipleship is love—gracious, generous, self-giving love.

That's the first "C," *communication*—physical, social, intellectual, and spiritual communication.

The Second "C" of a Great Marriage Is *Courtship*

It is so important, so crucial, to keep the courtship alive. In a marriage in the United States today, the married partners typically share four significant roles—breadwinners, homemakers, parents (in most instances, though not all), and lovers. Now, society plays a trick on us here. During the early courtship, the engagement, the wedding, and the honeymoon, society smiles and says, "Isn't that sweet? Look at that great couple—so in love! Isn't that wonderful?" But then, here's the trick. After the honeymoon, society turns on us: "No, no, no! Don't be too sweet to each other. You might lose control of your life. You might get henpecked. Don't be too sweet. Rather, you put bread on the table," society says. "That's how we are going to check you out. And you'd better have a nice, neat home or the neighbors and the city will march on your front door. And you'd better be good parents," society says, "or we will take your children away from you."

And at that point, nobody encourages us to be good lovers of each other. There is so much societal pressure to succeed at breadwinning and homemaking and parenting, that sometimes we use so much energy in those first three roles that we don't have any time or energy left over for the *courtship*, for the very thing that brought us together in the first place. Now, think about that. Most couples get together initially on the love and courtship level. I mean, for example, most guys would not walk into a crowded room and see a beautiful woman and say, "Wow! Wouldn't she be a great homemaker?" That is not where they are coming from. No, he is physically attracted—or she is physically attracted—and the flirtation begins, and the courtship begins.

Here's the point: all four of the roles are important. Be great breadwinners, be great homemakers, be great parents (if God blesses you with children); but in the process, don't lose each other. Keep courting, romancing, and loving each other. Make time for the courtship.

The first "C" of a great marriage is communication, and the second "C" of a great marriage is courtship.

The Third "C" of a Great Marriage Is *Commitment*

This means going into the marriage heart and soul, committed to the love, committed to the relationship, committed to the marriage, committed to each other. The mindset of commitment is so crucial. Let me show you why.

If you have the "trial-marriage" mindset, the "let's

9

try it and see if it works" mindset, then the first time there is a problem or some tension or some stress, your first thought is, *Well, I knew it wouldn't work, so I'll bail out now.* On the other hand, if you have the commitment mindset, then when stress comes, you simply say, "Oh, a little stress here. Let's see what this is about. Let's deal with this and grow on this and learn from this." You don't think about bailing out, because you are committed.

Now, let me put a footnote here. I know that some relationships become so destructive that you have no other choice but to dissolve them. But generally speaking, it is so crucial to go into the marriage with the commitment mindset.

The first "C" is communication, the second "C" is courtship, and the third "C" is commitment.

The Fourth "C" of a Great Marriage Is *Christ and His Church*

This is the most important "C" of all. When he was up in his years, William Barclay said something in a television interview that I thought was one of the greatest quotations I had ever heard outside of the Bible. Barclay said, "I'm an old man. I have lived a long time, and over the years I have learned that there are very few things in life that really matter . . . but those few things matter intensely." Isn't that a great quotation? "Few things in life really matter, but those few things matter intensely."

If you don't get elected second vice-president of the civic club, it's not the end of the world. It doesn't really matter that much. But what are the things that matter intensely? *Grace, honesty, integrity, kindness, justice, truth, morality, compassion, faith, hope,* and *love.* Now, wait a minute. Where have I heard all of those words before? I heard them at church. I learned them from the teaching of Jesus Christ. Even when I got them at home, they really came from Christ and the church, and those are the things that matter intensely. Those are the things that make a great marriage. Those are the things that make a great life, and they all came from Christ and his church!

One of the most beloved hymns of all time is "Blest Be the Tie That Binds." Well, Christ is the tie that binds. He is the One who unites and sustains "our hearts in Christian love."

2

In Real Estate, It's Location;
In Marriage, It's Communication

KEY FOCUS: This chapter offers some effective techniques for communicating well, including what to avoid.

Read John 1:1-5.

When our granddaughter, Sarah, was nine years old and in the third grade, she entered a project in her school's science fair. Her parents were pleased that she wanted to participate in the science fair, but they cautioned her not to get her hopes up too high for winning a ribbon, because she was entering the competition late. She started just two weeks before the deadline, whereas some of the other students had been planning and working on their projects for months.

Sarah's project was on buoyancy, the power that keeps things afloat. She wrote a daily journal about her scientific experiments. Sarah's journal was both informative and humorous. In addition to her scientific findings, she also included off-the-cuff remarks such as, "I have been working on this scientific project for two hours. I'm tired and I need a break. And besides that, one of my favorite TV programs is coming on right now. Bye-bye. I'll be back later." On another day, she wrote in her journal, "I have the flu today. I'm too tired and too weak to think about science now. Be back tomorrow."

Sarah prepared a colorful display using three large poster boards to depict her experiments on the subject of buoyancy. With bold blue letters, she entitled her display "What Floats Your Boat?" She turned in her project on a Wednesday. On Thursday, she was called in to answer questions from the panel of judges.

She wowed the judges with her ability to communicate. Many of the children were shy and embarrassed and frightened in front of the judges, but not Sarah! Sarah marched right into the room, she looked the judges square in the eye, and she said, "First, I think you would like to hear about the Archimedes Principle. Archimedes is called the 'Father of Buoyancy' because he was the one who discovered the force in nature that makes things float." She went on to show how her experiments proved that things do float, and that they float better in salt water than in regular tap water.

After her presentation, Sarah then answered all of the judges' questions with confidence. Finally, the judges asked her one last question: what did she want to be when she grew up? Sarah answered, "First, a singer. Then, a scientist!"

Later, her mother asked her, "Sarah, do you really want to be a scientist when you grow up?" Sarah replied, "Probably not. I just threw that in because I thought the judges wanted to hear that, and I thought it would make them feel good!"

The next morning it was announced that Sarah had won first place among the third graders, and she was awarded the blue ribbon. In their statement, the judges wrote that they liked her creative comments, both written and verbal, and they liked how confidently and boldly she was able to communicate her thoughts. At nine years of age, Sarah had already learned one of life's greatest lessons: the importance of communication.

Communication is so crucial, so significant, so consequential, so momentous, so vital! So, in this chapter, I want us to think together about "Communication in Marriage and the Family: Things to Avoid Like the Plague." Do you remember the old Henny Youngman joke about the man who went to the doctor one day? He said, "Look, Doc, every time I do my hand like this, it hurts." And the doctor said, "Well, don't do that!"

There are certain things in the family, in marriage, in our relationships with people that are so hurtful, so harmful, so destructive, that the only counsel is, "Don't do that! Don't do that anymore. It's too harmful; it's too hurtful."

Now, let me suggest some practical, effective Christian techniques for communicating, including some things that we need to beware of and avoid like the plague when we are trying to communicate.

First, Beware of Mind Games

What is a mind game? A mind game is a game we create in our minds to test someone's love for us or loyalty to us, when they don't know the game and they don't know that they are being tested. Mind games are unfair, and we should avoid them like the plague.

For example, I might think in my mind something like this: *If my daughter loves me, if she really loves me, then she will call me this afternoon at 2:00 PM.* But you see, that's unfair. She doesn't know that I'm wanting that or expecting that.

Or I might say, *If my son loves me, he will clean up his room before 5:00 PM!* Again, that's unfair. He doesn't know that's what I want. He doesn't know he is being tested.

Have you ever been with someone when everything is going along smoothly, and then all of a sudden the other person starts pouting or becomes angry with you or acts hurt? You feel like you have walked into the middle of a movie: *What* happened? *What did I* do? What happened was that someone played a mind game on you, and you didn't read that person's mind, and you didn't do what was expected. But, you see, that's unfair. How can you rise to the occasion if you don't know what the occasion is?

Let me give you a classic illustration of the silliness of mind games. Imagine that a young man and a young woman are going to have a romantic dinner—candlelight, nice music, just the two of them, gourmet hamburgers. They sit down at the beautifully appointed table; they hold hands; they have a prayer; and then the woman is hungry, so she quickly fixes her hamburger and begins eating. But the man notices the ketchup on the other side of the table, close to her. So, the man creates a mind game. He thinks, *She knows I like ketchup on my hamburgers. Why doesn't she pass me the ketchup? Look at her over there, feeding her face. I'm over here, starving. If she loved me, she would pass me the ketchup. She would be thinking of me. Well, I won't eat! I am just going to sit here and see how long it takes for her to realize that I need the ketchup!*

All of a sudden, she looks up and sees him pouting, moping, seething, and she can't figure it out, so she says to him, "Honey, is something wrong?" And he yells, "Do you have to ask?" And what started out as a nice, romantic evening becomes a scene, a disaster, a nightmare that could have been avoided so easily.

How? By the man simply saying, "Would you please pass the ketchup? I love ketchup on my hamburgers!" You see, it is so simple and yet so profound, because it works.

Some years ago I was doing a television interview with a psychologist, and I asked him, "What is the biggest problem in marriages and in families in America today?" Without hesitating, he said, "No question about it, the biggest problem in our families today is the crazy notion we have that if we have to ask for something—if we have to tell people what we are thinking, wanting, needing, or expecting—that it's second rate." He said, "Amazingly, we think if somebody loves us, they should be able to read our minds, and that if we have to say it, then it's second rate, and that's silly and unfair."

The point is, we have to tell each other what we are wanting, needing, feeling, thinking, and expecting. But let me hurry to say that we need to tell each other *tenderly* and *lovingly*.

Beware of mind games. They only lead to heartache, confusion, and sometimes disaster.

Second, Beware of Wrong Pronouns

The wrong pronoun is *you*—with a pointed finger. The right pronoun is *I*—with open hands.

When we say "you" with a pointed finger, communication immediately breaks down. When we say "I" with open hands, people lean forward to listen. The *you* pronoun is especially bad when we add the word *always* or *never*. "You always . . ." and "You never . . ." do not get a hearing or a response, only a negative reaction.

Let me show you what I mean. Now, suppose that my wife and I could put our daughter, Jodi, into a time machine and take her back to the time when she was sixteen years old. And imagine that sixteen-year-old Jodi wants to go to a party, but the rumor has gotten out that the party may be a bit wild, and she knows that I have heard the rumor. Now, here are two scenarios, where she first uses the wrong pronoun, and then uses the right pronoun.

Here is scenario number one, using the wrong pronoun—"you," with a pointed finger. Here is what happens. Jodi comes in and says, "Dad, I know you. I know how you are. I know what you think and what you are going to say, but I don't care what you say, I'm going to that party, and you can't stop me!"

What am I going to do? I'm going to think, *This*

young lady needs to be straightened out, and I'm going to list all of the reasons she shouldn't go to the party.

Here is scenario number two, using the right pronoun—"I," with open hands. Jodi comes to me and says, "Dad, I really need to talk with you for a few minutes about something that is really important to me. I want to go to this party Friday. It's so important to me, and let me try to explain why." (Then she gives me her reasons.) Then she says, "Now, I know about the rumors. I have heard them too, but I also know that I know how to act and that I can go to that party and have a good time, and I can do it in a way that will make my family proud of me." Why, in this scenario, I'll go fill up the car with gas for her, because she used the right pronoun!

It's so simple and yet so profound. Whenever we say "you" with a pointed finger, communication breaks down; and whenever we say "I" with open hands, people lean forward to listen. Try it this week, and you'll be amazed at what happens.

Third, Beware of Dumping Emotional Garbage on the Dinner Table

There is a time and place to talk about emotional things. In my opinion, dinnertime is not one of them. But you know what happens to us. We live at such a hectic, frantic pace that when we get to the dinner table, we think *now* we have a captive audience, so we go for the jugular.

There are times when we just need to love each other, and celebrate each other, and to be thankful to God for each other and for life and love. In the early days of the church, Holy Communion was a full meal where the church family came together to celebrate God's love and God's goodness, and their love for one another, and what they had in common and shared together. They communed with God and with one another in a spirit of peace, joy, gratitude, love, and celebration.

In the Christian home and in a Christian marriage, every meal should be that kind of holy communion—a time to celebrate, not a time to attack each other. A psychologist friend of mine illustrates this graphically. He says, "Imagine that you are having dinner with your family when all of a sudden, someone gets up, goes over and gets the garbage can, then comes back to the table and begins to drop garbage all around on the table."

That wouldn't be very appetizing, now, would it? Yet, that's what we do with emotional garbage, isn't it? We need to avoid that like the plague. Let dinnertime, let mealtime in the Christian home, be holy communion, where we celebrate God's love for us, and our love for God, and our love for each other.

21

Fourth, Beware of What We Put into Words

When God created the world, God spoke it into existence—"Let there be light"—and there was light. Now, listen! A lot of things get spoken into existence. If I say "I don't trust you" often enough, the reality is created. We can hurt people with words. We can punish people with words. We can make people sick with words. We can destroy people with words, so we need to be very careful about what we put into words.

The good news is on the other side of the coin: we can help and heal people with words. The words of encouragement, of appreciation, of kindness, of love can work incredible miracles. The point is clear: we only have so much breath, so use that breath to form words that build up, not words that tear down.

Beware of mind games, beware of wrong pronouns, beware of dumping emotional garbage on the dinner table, and beware of what you put into words.

Next, Beware of Misusing the First Four Minutes

Now, let me clarify this, because it is so important, and let me urge you to try it out this week. "The First Four Minutes" concept is the idea that the most important moments in any encounter are the first four minutes. Let me show you what I mean. In any interpersonal relationship (marriage, family, friendship, work, and so forth), two or more people come together. They are together, united, one, bonded. But then there are times when they go apart. They go to work, to school, to sleep, out of town; and then they come back together. They reenter the relationship, and the most significant time is the first four minutes of reentry. Why? Because deep down inside, all of us have insecure feelings, and we come back to the relationship wondering, *Is it still all right here for me? Am I still loved here? Am I still accepted? Am I still wanted here?*

As we reenter the relationship, we subconsciously want and need affirmation. So, when it comes to marriage, the first four minutes should be spent in affirming each other, loving each other, hugging each other, kissing each other, welcoming each other, celebrating each other. If we affirm each other for four minutes, then no one feels personally attacked if later we have to deal with problems.

So, when I come home (if you arrive before I do, and if you've been waiting for me) . . .

Love me for four minutes, and *then* tell me I'm late.

Love me for four minutes, and *then* ask me where I've been.

Love me for four minutes, and *then* tell me the dog broke our favorite lamp.

Love me for four minutes, and *then* tell me that the crew from *60 Minutes* is in the den and that they want to talk to me.

Love me for four minutes, and *then* show me the letter from the Internal Revenue Service!

Now, this is true for every human being. We all need the first four minutes of love and affirmation. Children need it, wives need it, husbands need it, mothers need it, fathers need it, friends need it, co-workers need it. Everybody needs it—just four minutes of encouragement and acceptance. It is so important. Try it this week, and you will be amazed.

Finally, Beware of Neglecting God and the Church

I don't know nearly as much about communicating as I would like to know, but what little I do know, I learned at the church. What does it take to communicate well in marriage? Love, respect, thoughtfulness, patience, tenderness, compassion, empathy, gratitude, effort, commitment. I don't know nearly as much as I would like to know about those great qualities, but what little I do know about them, I learned from God at the church.

In the prologue to John's Gospel, Jesus is called the Word of God. What does that mean? Simply this: Jesus was God's idea for us, God's plan for us, God's truth for us wrapped up in a person. God's Word became flesh and dwelt among us. He came to show us what God is like and what God wants us to be like.

So, Jesus is the measuring stick for communicating. He is the pattern, the model, the example, the blueprint. And when Jesus spoke, people heard and saw and felt God. That's our calling, isn't it? To so speak that people can hear through our frail words and actions the eternal Word of God. To so speak that our words fill the air—not with the sounds of hate and hostility; not with the sounds of temper or cruelty; not with the sounds of jealousy or vengeance or self-pity; but with the words of life, the words of grace, the words of love.

3
Celebrating the Gift of Marriage

KEY FOCUS: If you want to have a joyful, celebrative marriage, don't be crabby, critical, or controlling.

Read John 13:34-35.

They said it couldn't be done. They said it was physically impossible. They said it would never happen, but on May 6, 1954, a young medical student named Roger Bannister did it: he ran a mile in under four minutes!

For centuries, as far back as the athletic games in ancient Greece, many people believed that the human being could not break the four-minute mile. Medical doctors and physiologists had determined that the human body was so constructed that it would be physically impossible to run a mile in less than four minutes. Our bone structure was all wrong for it, they said. The wind resistance was too great. Our lung capacity was inadequate to accomplish this amazing feat. There was just one problem with that conclusion: they forgot to tell Roger Bannister. Or, at least, they didn't convince him.

And so at the Iffley Road Track in Oxford on a wet and windy day, May 6, 1954, with 3,000 people watching, Great Britain's Roger Bannister did the unthinkable. He ran a mile in 3 minutes, 59.4 seconds and, of course, established a new world record—a new world record that lasted, interestingly, for only forty-six days.

Forty-six days later, John Landy of Australia lowered the record to 3:58. The astonishing thing is that after Roger Bannister broke the four-minute-mile barrier, thirty-seven other runners accomplished it in the months that followed; and since that time, a total of 955 runners have done it. Just nine years after Roger Bannister's historic run, Jim Ryan accomplished a sub-four-minute mile while still in high school.

The current world record holder, as of this writing, is Hicham El Guerrouj of Morocco. He ran the mile in 3 minutes, 43 seconds, and at that pace, he would have finished 120 yards ahead of Roger Bannister.

They said it couldn't be done, but once one runner did it, the sub-four-minute mile over time became a rather commonplace occurrence in the world of track and field. John McDonnell is the track coach at the University of Arkansas. In his years of coaching, more than twenty of his runners have broken the four-minute mile.

Now, what does this have to do with us, and what does it have to do with marriage? Just this: It dramatically shows us that when people believe something can be done, when people know that something can be done, it opens the door of possibility for them. It raises the bar of their expectations, and rather than say, "It can't be done," they say, "I can do that too."

With that in mind, let me tell you that in our church family just a few years ago, we had 116 couples who had been married for 50 years or longer. Of these 116 couples, 22 of the couples had been married for more than 60 years. The point is, it can be done, and when we know that it's doable, then we can with more confidence strive to accomplish that feat.

Now, let me hurry to say what we all know: there are some situations that somehow become so painful, so destructive, and sometimes even so dangerous, that the only answer is to dissolve the relationship, to learn from it and move on and make a new beginning with your life. And if that happens, you can know that God loves you and God is with you, and that the church is here with incredible resources to support you and encourage you, and to help you shape a new beginning.

Apart from those hurtful situations, it is doable; couples can make it work. But the key word here is *work*. We have to work at it. As someone once said, "Good marriages are made in heaven, but they have to be worked out here on earth."

So, let me share some ideas with you about this. Over the years, I have visited with many, many married couples, some happy and some not so happy, and I have learned through those conversations and experiences that there are certain predictable, insidious, negative things that can sour the relationship and poison the marriage. These same problems crop up over and over again, and the bottom line is that we are better off not doing these things.

So, here they are. If you want to have a happy, healthy marriage and a joyful relationship, here are three things you need to avoid like the plague—three things *not* to do!

First of All, Don't Be Crabby

In the "Peanuts" comic strip, Lucy is the queen of crabbiness. She loves to rain on other people's parade. Once, her little brother, Linus, drew a cartoon. He was so proud of it. He wanted Lucy to look at it and compliment it, and to be proud of him. Lucy said, "Who drew it?" Linus replied, "I drew it." And Lucy said, "If you drew it, then I think it's *terrible*!"

Dejected, Linus walked away, saying, "Big sisters are the crabgrass in the lawn of life!"

Lucy always pulls the football away when Charlie Brown is trying to kick it, causing Charlie Brown to fall and land on his back. Lucy always gripes and complains. She is always crabby. Now, this may be funny in Charles Schulz's classic and beloved comic strip, but you wouldn't want to be married to Lucy. It's not fun to be around crabby people.

But let me hurry to say that crabbiness is no respecter of genders. Men can be crabby and women can be crabby. But as Christians, we should not be crabby!

Christianity is by definition "responsive gratitude." As Christians we are grateful to God for the gift of life, and we are grateful to God for the incredible gift of eternal and abundant life that we have because of the sacrificial love of Jesus Christ. Gratitude, appreciation, thankfulness, joy, love, kindness, graciousness, tenderness, compassion, humility: these are key marks of the Christian, not grouchiness.

But unfortunately, sometimes we forget that, and we give in to anger and cynicism and pessimism and selfishness. When that happens, we can become grumpy and crabby, and then our prevailing spirit is to fuss and gripe and complain about everything.

Some years ago, a young pastor in Scotland was

sent to a new church. Now, there was a woman in that church named Mrs. McTavish, who seemed to have been born in the "objective" mood. That is, she was against everything. She never agreed with anybody on anything. She was stubborn and harsh and bitter about everything, and she seemed always to be in a bad mood.

One Sunday morning, she and the young pastor clashed. Hard words were spoken. Later, the young pastor felt sorry and sad. He had said some things he regretted. So, he went to her home to apologize and to ask for forgiveness. As he approached her apartment, he saw Mrs. McTavish looking out the window, so he knew she was home.

The pastor went up to the door and rang the bell; no response. He knocked on the door; no response. He knocked louder and called out the woman's name; still no response.

The pastor then proceeded to do something no minister should ever do: he stooped down on one knee and looked through the keyhole. Well, it just so happened that Mrs. McTavish had done the same thing on her side of the door at the same time. As their eyes met through the keyhole, the young pastor said, "Well, well, Mrs. McTavish, this is the first time that you and I have seen eye-to-eye on anything!"

Then Mrs. McTavish opened the door and did something the pastor never had seen her do before:

She smiled! And then she laughed loudly. The young pastor laughed with her and asked for forgiveness. She took his hand warmly and invited him in for tea. She told him she was sorry too, and that she didn't mean to be so cantankerous. Then she said, "I guess I'm just lonely. You are the first person to come see me since my husband died more than ten years ago."

The point is, Mrs. McTavish had not always been crabby. She had become overwhelmed by her problems, and in the process, she lost her gratitude, she lost her joy, she lost her sense of humor. Please don't let that happen to you. If you feel disillusioned with life, get help. The gift of life and love is too precious to waste in crabbiness.

Some years ago, I was working with a middle-aged couple who were having serious marriage problems. One day the man said to me, "Sure, I talk tough to her, but she can take it. Everybody knows I was born with a hot temper. I say hard things to her all the time, but she knows how I am . . . she understands." And I had to tell him, "No, she *doesn't*! She *doesn't* understand. Again and again, day after day, week after week, she comes to the church crying, and saying, 'How can he love me and talk to me like that?'"

Time after time over the years I have seen it—that crabby, grumpy attitude tearing marriages apart. So, that's number one: Don't be crabby! Be grateful!

Second, Don't Be Critical

Especially, don't be *contemptuously* critical, and don't give advice. As someone once said, "Don't give advice. Wise folks don't need it; fools won't heed it!" We only have so much breath, so why not use that breath to form words that build people up instead of words that tear people down?

In French, the word *encourage* means literally "to put the heart in." The word *discourage* means "to tear the heart out." In the Christian home, we should go overboard in saying words that encourage and affirm and reassure, not words that tear people down. A poet put it like this: "A good thing to remember and a better thing to do, is to work with the construction gang, and not with the wrecking crew."

Besides that, all of us have way too many faults of our own to be harshly and arrogantly and contemptuously critical of others. We all have sinned and fallen short of the glory of God. Besides that, it is so much more rewarding, so much more loving, and so much more fun to encourage our loved ones than to cut them down with critical words, contemptuous body language, and actions that wound and devastate and break the heart.

A famous minister had a two o'clock appointment with a man he never had met before. The man wanted counseling. When the minister returned from lunch at 1:45, he received an emergency call about a death in the church family. He took the call, as he should have, but it made him four minutes late for his two o'clock counseling appointment. When the minister walked in to the counseling office, the waiting man immediately took the minister to task. "You are four minutes late for our appointment," the man said. "Let me give you a little advice: be on time. It was rude of you to keep me waiting like this."

The minister apologized and asked for forgiveness for his tardiness, and then the minister said, "How may I be of service to you?" And the man said, "I have trouble sustaining a relationship. People don't seem to enjoy being around me for some reason." The minister measured his words and said, "Well, you know, you and I had never met until today, and you were pretty harsh with me because I was a few minutes late. I didn't tell you before, but the reason I was late was because I had an emergency call. A good friend's mother just died, and I was trying to help this friend, and the call took a little longer than I had anticipated. People don't enjoy being fussed at or criticized, and maybe that's why they pull away from you. It's always best to be gracious. It's always best to cut people a little slack. It's always best to be kind. It's always best to be loving."

That minister was right, wasn't he? So, if you want a marriage that will mature and grow and sustain and deepen; if you want it to be fun and joyful and tender and beautiful, then first, don't be crabby—be grateful; and second, don't be critical—be respectful.

Third and Finally, Don't Be Controlling

In a marriage, it is so important, so crucial, to remember that you don't always have to be in charge; that you don't always have to be in control; that you don't always have to make every decision.

That's the beauty of marriage. It's a shared relationship, a shared wisdom, a shared love. Sometimes people forget that, and they try to take control. Their motto is "My Way or the Highway." They don't even realize that in so doing, they are implying to their mate, "I'm smarter than you," "I don't trust your judgment," "I don't think you have a lick of sense." And that is not the Christian spirit.

It is so important to keep the courtship alive in a marriage, and this control tactic is a great enemy of love and courtship. As I mentioned in a previous chapter, society plays a terrible trick on us here. During the early courtship, the engagement, the wedding, and the honeymoon, society smiles and says, "Isn't that sweet? Look at that great couple—so in love. Isn't that wonderful?"

But then, after the honeymoon, society turns on us and says, "Hold on! Don't be too sweet to each other.

You might get henpecked. Don't be too sweet to each other. You might lose control of your life!"

I heard a psychologist talking about this on television. Referring to her own marriage, she summed it up like this: "During the courtship, I was scared to death that I was going to lose him. After the honeymoon, I was scared to death that I was going to lose *me*."

What's the answer? Simply this: Keep the courtship alive by getting up in the morning and going to bed at night thinking, *How can I bring joy and happiness and pleasure and support to this life-mate of mine whom I love so much?* If you have two people doing that at the same time, you have heaven on earth.

Once I ran across an article on marriage in a magazine. It was pretty routine, but it had one great line in it that touched my soul. It read, "If you ever find yourself in a situation where you can either make yourself look good or your mate look good, always choose to make your mate look good."

That is so true—and so Christian. Now, you may be wondering when I'm going to get to our biblical text for this chapter, so here it comes. In John 13:34-35, Jesus said, "A new commandment I give to you, that you love one another; even as I have loved you" (RSV).

Notice, now, that Jesus did not just say, "Love one another." He said, "Love one another; even as I have loved you." That is the key to a great Christian marriage—two people loving each other in the way Christ loved: generously, graciously, compassionately, sacrificially, unconditionally. That's the way to make a marriage work and last and be joyful and celebrative—to love each other with a Christlike spirit, with a Christlike love.

One morning, a Sunday-school teacher told her fifth graders the story of Jesus' first miracle. It happened at a wedding in Cana of Galilee. After the teacher finished telling the story, she asked her class, "Now, what do we learn from this story?" A little boy raised his hand and said, "I learned that when you have a wedding, it's a good idea to have Jesus there!"

Indeed so! And when you have a marriage, it's a good idea to have Jesus there, because Jesus reminds us not to be crabby, but to be grateful; not to be critical, but to be respectful; and not to be controlling, but to be gracious.

4
Happy Marriage:
It's All about Choices

KEY FOCUS: In living and in marriage, often our choices control our outcomes.

Read Matthew 5:9.

The power mower broke down and wouldn't run, and the grass in the front yard was getting totally out of hand. The wife was embarrassed about the way the lawn looked, so she began hinting to her husband that it was time to get the power mower fixed. But somehow her hints didn't work. The message never sank in.

Finally, she thought of a clever way to make her point: when her husband arrived home one day, he found her seated in the tall grass on the front lawn, fussily snipping away (one blade of grass at a time) with a tiny pair of sewing scissors.

The husband watched her for a few minutes, and then he went into the house. Soon he came back with a toothbrush. He handed it to her and said, "When you get through, you might want to sweep the sidewalks!" The doctors say that man will walk again, but he will probably always have a limp!

Now, there is a sermon there somewhere, and it has to do with the importance and the power of communication, and how what we communicate and the way we communicate it can have a dramatic impact on other people.

It can bring joy or sorrow, gladness or sadness.

It can pick people up or knock them down.

What we communicate can bring pleasure or pain.

We can be peacemakers or heartbreakers.

Over the years, I have come to realize something that I think is incredibly important, namely this: that in living each day, we have a choice.

We can build up or we can tear down, and the happy people in life are those who realize that we have that choice and then, with the help of God, consciously choose to build up.

This, of course, is what the seventh beatitude is about. When Jesus said, "Blessed are the peacemakers, for they will be called children of God" (Matthew 5:9), what he meant was, "How happy and fulfilled are the peacemakers, for they are doing a Godlike work!" There is nothing in the world more Godlike than peacemaking.

Commenting on this beatitude, William Barclay pointed out:

> There are people who are always storm-centers of trouble and bitterness and strife. Wherever they are, they are either involved in quarrels themselves or the cause of quarrels between others. They are trouble-makers. There are people like that in almost every society . . . and such people are doing the devil's own work.
>
> On the other hand—thank God—there are people in whose presence bitterness cannot live, people who bridge the gulfs, and heal the breaches, and sweeten the bitternesses. Such people are doing a God-like work, for it is the great purpose of God to bring peace between men and himself and man to man. The man who divides men is doing the devil's work; the man who unites men is doing God's work. (William Barclay, *Commentary on Matthew*, page 110)

In marriage and in life, the choice is yours: you can be a troublemaker or a peacemaker. You can build up or you can tear down! Let me illustrate and amplify the point with three ideas, and maybe we can find ourselves somewhere between the lines.

First of All, the Choice Is Yours: You Can Encourage or You Can Discourage

There is a strange sentence in one of the psalms: "I will keep my mouth with a bridle!" (39:1 KJV). These are the words of a man sorely tempted to spread gloom and despair and discouragement. Yet he held himself in check, knowing that there was enough pessimism around. He knew that he needed to help rally the courage of those who felt down and out.

That's good advice for all of us. The world has its share of cynics and debunkers. It is longing for words of assurance and encouragement. When will we ever learn? People don't want to be put down; they are crying out to be lifted up.

What have you been choosing lately? The choice is yours: you can encourage or you can discourage. In thinking of this, I remembered some lines written long ago by R. L. Sharpe:

Isn't it strange
That princes and kings
And clowns that caper
In sawdust rings,
And common people
Like you and me
Are builders for eternity?

Each is given a bag of tools,
A shapeless mass,
A book of rules;
And each must make,
Ere life is flown,
A stumbling-block
Or a stepping stone.

Isn't it sad that so many people have gotten it mixed up? They have turned it completely around. They think they are divinely ordained to point out all the bad things and to show us all the problems and to underscore all the negatives.

Some years ago, I was appointed to serve a church in a small town in west Tennessee. My wife, June, and I moved into the parsonage at noon on a Thursday. My predecessor, the Reverend Larry Yates, had moved out just a few minutes before. At 12:15 PM (we had been there only fifteen minutes), the doorbell rang. It was a woman who was a member of the church, who felt that it was her duty to come and tell me about all the problems in the church, and especially to point out all the things Brother Yates had done wrong. On and on she went, spreading her message of despair and gloom and saying terrible things about her former pastor.

As this woman intoned her discouraging words, and as I listened to her "words of woe," I remember thinking three things. First, I thought, *Lady, you are telling me a lot more about yourself than about Brother Yates.* Second, I thought, *I have known Larry Yates for years, and he's great. I don't believe these awful things she is saying about him.* And third, I thought, *One of these days, I'm going to be leaving here, and this woman is going to be here by noon to tell my successor all about me and my faults.*

Isn't that tragic? Why do we feel that we have to spread gloom? It is so much more fun to lift people up rather than tear them down.

In Laura Huxley's book *You're Not the Target*, the author puts it well when she says:

> At one time or another the more fortunate among us make three startling discoveries.
> Discovery Number One: Each one of us has, in varying degree, the power to make others feel better or worse.
> Discovery Number Two: Making others feel better is much more rewarding than making them feel worse.
> Discovery Number Three: Making others feel better generally makes us feel better. (New York: Farrar, Straus & Co., 1972; page 3)

One of the great personalities of the early church was a man named Barnabas. That's a great name, Barnabas, because it means "the child of encouragement." Barnabas was a significant leader of the New

Testament church because he lived out his name; he was an encourager.

We in the church ought to be modern-day "Barnabases," the sons and daughters of encouragement; people who listen, who care, who affirm; people who help one another and support one another; people who lift up and build up.

But, the choice is yours: you can encourage or you can discourage!

Second, the Choice Is Yours: You Can Laugh or You Can Lament

Some people go miserably through life crying, "Woe is me!" lamenting at every turn. This is sad, because God meant life to be joyous. A good sense of humor has never hurt a single person, and it has made life blossom like a flower in the desert for many.

Sir Max Beerbohm once wrote, "Strange when you think of it, that of all the countless folk who have lived before our time on this planet not one is known in history or legend as having died of laughter." And Abraham Lincoln once said, "With the fearful strain that is on me night and day, if I did not laugh from time to time I would surely die." How important it is to learn not to take yourself so seriously, and to learn how to laugh.

I perform a lot of weddings. It is interesting to watch people go through weddings. It's a nervous, emotional time, and those with a sense of humor, those who know how to laugh, fare so much better.

Some years ago, I performed a wedding that turned into a disaster because the bride had no sense of humor. She was determined to have "the ultimate, perfect wedding." But she tried too hard and got everybody so upset that everything went wrong. Everything she had ever heard of, she put into this wedding: bridesmaids and groomsmen, acolytes and altar boys, flower girls and ring bearers. Everything went along okay until the end. When the time came for the nuptial kiss, as a surprise to the rest of us, she wanted her brother to play—of all things—the *2001: A Space Odyssey* theme on his stereo tape recorder. The music came on too loud, so loud that it startled everyone. The maid of honor jumped and knocked over a candle. As the best man tried to catch the falling candle, he stepped on the bride's dress. The bride dropped her flowers, and her veil fell off. She stumbled as she was walking up the aisle of the church, and then the flower girl began to cry and scream. By the time the bride and groom got to the back of the church, the bride was furious, and she had decided that it was all the groom's fault! She was so mad at him, and he couldn't figure out what he had done wrong.

That was the only time in my life that I had to take the bride and groom off into a private room and calm them down before they could even go into the reception. I said to them, "Look, you are married. That's all that matters. You love each other, and you want to share all of life together, and you are just as married as any couple who has ever taken those sacred vows. That's what it's all about! All the candles and pageantry, that's just frosting on the cake. There are no perfect weddings, and the things that went wrong are just things to laugh about and have fun with for years to come. You love each other, and you are married; *that's* the important thing."

Put that over against this. There is another couple I know who had one of the most unusual wedding experiences I know of. We accidentally scheduled their wedding in our church sanctuary on the same day and time as a parade that began in our church parking lot. The streets were blocked off, and no one could get to the church. At the appointed time for the wedding, we had no congregation; the guests couldn't get there because of the parade. So, we had to delay the wedding for a full hour.

What do you do when things like that happen? Well, you can laugh or you can lament! That great couple that Saturday evening decided to laugh. Their sense of humor got them through. They went out and had their picture made with the parade bands, and they still joke about how at their wedding they had an hour-long parade with seventeen marching bands!

Or what about the couple getting married in Arkansas? The minister asked the groom, "Will you have this woman to be your wedded wife, to live together in the holy estate of matrimony? Will you love her, comfort her, honor and keep her, in sickness and in health; and, forsaking all others, keep you only unto her, so long as you both shall live?" The groom was so nervous that he answered, "Would you repeat the question?"

It took a sense of humor for that couple to get through that. They have it on tape, and every now and then, to this day, they listen to it and laugh!

Well, what do you think? The choice is yours: you can encourage or you can discourage; you can laugh or you can lament.

Third and Finally, the Choice Is Yours: You Can Pardon or You Can Punish

Why do we think we need to punish people? Every time I see that bumper sticker that reads *I don't get mad; I get even!* it makes me feel so sad.

Some time ago, a man came by to see me. He was depressed and despondent. He and his wife were having problems. The weekend before, they had gone to San Antonio to celebrate their anniversary. As they were heading out of town he remembered something he had forgotten to take care of at his office. He made a quick detour, went to his office, made the necessary arrangements, and they were on their way, having lost only fifteen minutes with their stop.

But for some reason, the stop made his wife furious. The couple drove to San Antonio in silence. They endured a miserable weekend. She refused to speak to him. When he tried to talk, she turned away. When he tried to touch her, she pushed him away.

A week had passed when he came to see me. "She still won't speak to me," he said. "She won't listen to reason. She is still punishing me."

Isn't that sad? Isn't that tragic? Why do we punish people? Why do we punish those we love in such cruel ways? It is so useless. It is so senseless! It is so ridiculous!

It is so much better to pardon!

It is so much better to forgive!

It is so much better to be a peacemaker!

Well, the choice is yours: in marriage and in life, you can encourage or you can discourage; you can laugh or you can lament; you can pardon or you can punish.

5
The Church in Your House

KEY FOCUS: The Christian home should be where love of God and love of others is first expressed and lived out.

Read Philemon 1-7.

Have you heard the story about the barber who had a negative attitude about everything? This barber was always whining, always complaining, always grumbling. He always saw the cup as being half empty. He was just cynical and negative about everything.

One day a man came to his barbershop to get a haircut. The man got into the chair. He said he was so excited because he was going to make a wonderful trip to Europe and would be leaving the very next day.

The negative barber asked, "Where are you going?"

The man said, "First, we are going to go to London."

The barber interrupted him and said, "London? Oh, that's a terrible place. It's dirty and noisy and way too expensive. You won't like it there in London. Where else are you going?"

"Well, we are going to go over to Paris."

"Oh my goodness, Paris is *worse*. The people there are really very rude. You won't like it in Paris. Where else are you going?"

"Next, we are going to fly to Rome."

"Oh, Rome is the worst of all. The food is terrible. And whatever you do, don't visit the Vatican. The lines are too long. And don't think you are going to see the pope, either, because the pope is not accessible. And even if you do see him, you won't understand a word he says, because he doesn't speak English."

Well, the next day the man went on his trip. Two weeks later he returned to the negative barber for another haircut. The barber asked: "How was your trip?"

The man said, "It was absolutely terrific. London was great. It was the most exciting city, and we found the prices really quite reasonable. Paris was a beautiful city, very hospitable. Everyone was kind to us, and Rome was the perfect climax to our trip. Everything was wonderful. We went to the Vatican and even had an audience with the pope. There weren't any crowds there at all. It was like a private audience with the pope, and he spoke to each of us personally, in English. He had me kneel, placed his hand upon my head, and gave me a blessing. Then, he leaned forward and spoke into my ear, in perfect English, these words: 'You are a very handsome man, but I have to tell you: you have the *worst haircut* I have ever seen in my life!'"

Now, that old story teaches us two things: first, a negative attitude is not a pretty picture; and second, our negative attitudes can come back to haunt us. Sometimes a negative, cynical, critical, complaining attitude is just irritating and annoying, as we see in that negative, grumpy barber. But sadly, sometimes such an attitude gets pushed too far in some people, and destructive things happen. Marriages are dissolved and families are torn apart. Somebody's expectations are not met, and if the persons involved fail to talk about this and/or get help, disillusionment sets in and begins to poison the spirit and the relationship. Negative thoughts creep in. Brooding resentment takes root and festers and fumes. Communication breaks down. Affection grows cold. Then all of these harbored, stored-up, hostile feelings explode in an emotional scene (or just quietly, but surely, drive the persons involved further apart), and hearts are broken, and persons who once loved each other so much suddenly feel like strangers. What was once a beautiful, constructive relationship, with high hopes for a bright future, has now become a destructive, painful one.

These kinds of negative experiences not only push people into divorce court, but they also remind us graphically how important it is, how essential it is that we get back to making Christian marriage and the Christian home a top and urgent priority. The Christian home should be the very first place where we learn not to be negative, but to celebrate life as a precious gift from God. The Christian home should be the very first place where we learn the difference between right and wrong.

The Christian home should be the very first place where we learn how to share and how to respect others. The Christian home should be the very first place where we learn how to pray and where we hear the stories of Jesus. The Christian home should be the very first place where we learn to be loved and to love. The Christian home should be the very first place where we learn how not to be hostile and negative, but rather to say yes to life, yes to other people, yes to the church, and yes to God.

Sometimes we forget that. Sometimes in our rush to succeed, we put that on the back burner and neglect our marriages and our home life.

Clovis Chappell, a noted minister from an earlier

day, used to tell the story of two paddleboats. They left Memphis about the same time, traveling down the Mississippi River to New Orleans. As they traveled side by side, some sailors from one boat made a few derogatory remarks about the slow pace of the other boat. Words were exchanged, challenges were made, and the race began. The competition became vicious as the two boats roared through the Deep South.

One boat began falling behind—not enough fuel. There had been plenty of coal for the trip, but not enough for a race. As the boat dropped back, an enterprising young sailor took some of the ship's cargo and tossed it into the ovens. When the other sailors on his boat saw that these supplies burned as well as the coal, they got excited, and they quickly fueled their boat with the cargo they had been assigned to transport. They ended up winning the race—but in the process, they burned up all of their precious cargo!

Now, there is a sermon there somewhere, because, you see, God has entrusted some special and precious cargo to us: our spouses, our children, our grandchildren, our friends, our neighbors, our church, and our own souls. Our job is to do our part in seeing that this cargo reaches its destination. But when the Rat Race, the rush to success, takes priority over people (especially those in the family), then people suffer, people get hurt, and sometimes marriages are lost and homes are disrupted. Think of it. How much cargo do we sacrifice in order to achieve the number-one slot? How many people never reach the destination because of the aggressiveness of a competitive captain?

Jesus warned us about this. He said, "What will it profit a man"—or a woman, or a family, or a nation—"if he gains the whole world, and loses his own soul?" What does it profit to win the Rat Race but lose your precious cargo? The point is clear: we must get back to emphasizing and cultivating Christian marriage and the Christian home.

In our scripture for this chapter, we find Paul writing a letter to his Christian friend Philemon, and in the letter Paul sends greetings "to the church in your house." Isn't that a fascinating phrase, "the church in your house"? That's the way they had to do it in the early church, through the "house church." They didn't have gothic cathedrals or Georgian sanctuaries. They didn't have church buildings at all. The early Christians met in homes. And you know, that's still relevant for us today, because every Christian home should be a "house church," and every Christian marriage should be a relationship rooted in God.

With that in mind, let me ask you: What does the church in your house look like? What are the things that define a Christian marriage and a Christian home? Let me suggest three, and I'm sure you will think of others.

First of All, a Christian Home Is a Place Where the Truth of Christ Is Embraced

When we know the truth, it will indeed set us free. However, the problem is that sometimes it is very difficult to sort out what is true. This is particularly the case in our time. How do we tell what is true and what is propaganda, or what is a blatant lie?

There's an old Native American legend that sums up the situation powerfully. It tells of a Native American boy who climbed to the top of a tall mountain to prove his manhood. When he reached the highest peak of the mountain, he was very proud of what he had accomplished. He looked out far and wide and felt as though he was on top of the world. But then the boy heard a sound at his feet. He looked down and saw a deadly snake. Before he could move, the snake spoke to him. "I am about to die," said the snake. "It's too cold for me up here, and there is no food. Put me under your shirt and take me down to the warmth of the valley."

"Oh no," said the young boy. "I know your kind. You are a rattlesnake. If I pick you up, you will bite me, and your poisonous bite will kill me."

"Not so," said the snake. "I will treat you

differently. If you do this for me, I will never harm you. I'll be your best friend."

The youth resisted for a while, but the snake was very persuasive. At last, the young boy gave in and tucked the rattlesnake under his shirt. He carried it down to the valley, and there he laid it down gently. Suddenly, the snake coiled, rattled, and struck, biting the boy on the leg.

"But, you promised!" cried the young man.

"You knew what I was when you picked me up," said the snake, as it slithered away. (See *Guideposts*, July 1988; and *Reader's Digest*, June 1989, page 131.)

That's a blunt but powerful parable for us, isn't it? The point is clear: we can be tricked. We can be confused. We can be duped.

If we pick up the serpent of aggression or ruthlessness, it will eventually bite us. If we carry the serpent of hate or prejudice, ultimately it will poison us. If we embrace the serpent of selfishness, it will strike us and bring us down.

But how do we know what's right? How do we keep from being taken in? With all of the conflicting ideas bombarding us today and vying for our allegiance, how do we know the truth?

Well, we need a fixed point for truth. We need a measuring stick, and that is one thing Jesus Christ does for us very well. He is our measuring stick for truth.

In the prologue to John's Gospel, Jesus is referred to as the Word of God. The Greek word is *logos*, and it means the will of God, the mind of God, the idea of God, the purpose of God, the intention of God, or, put another way, the truth of God.

If we want to know how wide something is, there is only one way to know for sure: we measure it with a dependable measuring stick. That's what Jesus Christ does for us. He is the measuring stick for truth. We need to measure everything we see or read or hear by the standard of truth we see in Jesus Christ.

If we hear someone speak words that are mean-spirited, shout words that are hateful, scream words that are cruel, mutter words that are prejudiced, spew out words that are profane, then we can be sure that they don't measure up to the test of Jesus Christ. Jesus is the measuring stick for truth, and his truth is a fixed point we can always count on.

That's number one: The truth of Christ is a major emphasis in a Christian marriage and in the Christian home. The Christian home is a place where the truth of Christ is embraced.

Second, a Christian Home Is a Place Where Love Is Expressed

Love is another fixed point in the Christian home that we can always trust. Jesus taught that emphatically, in word and in deed. In the way he lived and in the way he died, he epitomized the power of love.

If we in our marriages, in our homes, and in this world could somehow capture the spirit of Christ, if we could all learn to live together in love and goodwill, just think what we could do, just think what we could accomplish.

When the famous writer F. Scott Fitzgerald died, he left among his papers the plot of a play, which he never wrote. It was a simple story about five people who lived in various parts of the world. They all inherited one house. However, there was a condition: they all had to live together in that house! Without question, this is the plot for our shrinking world today; and without question, the hope for our world today is found in Jesus Christ and in the love he embodied. He shows us what God is like and what God wants us to be like, and the word is *love!*

You are probably familiar with the name Babe Ruth. He was one of the greatest baseball players of all time. "The Babe," as he was affectionately called, hit 714 home runs during his baseball career. But unfortunately, he played too long. He continued to play when he had gotten older and his ability had waned, both at bat and in the field.

During one of his last games as a professional, the aging Babe Ruth had a terrible day. He made several errors. In just one inning, his errors were responsible for the five runs scored by the opposing team. As Babe Ruth walked off the field after that disastrous inning and headed for the dugout, a crescendo of boos and catcalls was directed at him by the angry crowd. Babe Ruth had never known a moment like that. The fans who had loved him for so many years had turned on him with a vengeance. It was a painful and humiliating moment for this great athlete, who had been the number-one star of baseball for so long.

But just then, a little boy in the bleachers couldn't stand it. He couldn't bear seeing Babe Ruth hurt like that. The little boy jumped over the railing, onto the playing field, and with tears streaming down his face he ran toward Babe Ruth. He knelt before his hero and threw his arms around the player's legs. Babe Ruth picked the little boy up and hugged him tightly.

Suddenly, the noise from the stands came to an abrupt stop. There was no more booing. In fact, an incredible hush fell over the entire ballpark. The boy's love for Babe Ruth had melted the hearts of that hostile crowd. Love happened in right field, and suddenly the outcome of a baseball game didn't seem that important anymore. (See Brian Cavanaugh, *The Sower's Seeds* [Mahwah, N.J.: Paulist Press, 1990].)

Where did that little boy learn to love like that? Probably at home and at church. Love is another fixed point for the Christian home and for Christian marriage in this changing world. It's something we can always trust and always count on. It brings us back to reality.

Finally, a Christian Home Is a Place Where God Is Honored

God, of course, is the most important fixed point of all. God is the one constant that we can always depend on in our marriages and in our homes and in all of our relationships.

Years ago, the great preacher Phillips Brooks used to lean over the pulpit at Harvard and say to those young students: "Young people, commit your life to God, believe in him, lean on him, and in the last analysis nothing will ever overcome you."

Some years ago, I went to visit with a couple who were facing a very difficult challenge. The husband, who had been so strong for so many years, had been in an automobile accident. His legs were injured severely, and he and his devoted wife had just been given the news that he would likely never be able to walk again without assistance and might be confined to a wheelchair for the rest of his life.

It was a hard pill to swallow for this dedicated couple, but they never wavered in their faith and in their trust in God. And, as always, they were an inspiration to everyone with their beautiful love for each other. As he sat up in his hospital bed in obvious pain, but still with a radiant smile on his face, his wife sat on the edge of the bed with her loving and supportive arms wrapped around him. Tears were misting her eyes. He patted her hands and said, "Honey, don't you worry now. We have been through a lot together over the years and God has been with us every step of the way, and God will be with us in this inconvenience. I'm going to do everything I can to get up on my feet and walk again, and I truly believe I will with God's help, but even if I don't," he said, pointing to his wheelchair, "I've got wheels! Don't worry. God will see us through!"

Let me ask you something: Is your faith that strong? Do you trust God like that? That couple had experienced the presence of God in their life together many times before, in times of joy and sorrow, in times of victory and disappointment, in good times and in hard times, and they knew that would God would be with them again in this new and difficult situation. They were confident of that.

In Philippians 4:13, The Apostle Paul says, "I can do all things through him who strengthens me." I had a seminary professor some years ago who said that what this means is "I'm ready for anything! Bring it on, for God is my strength!"

Occasionally our church's choir sings the anthem "My God and I." In that anthem, there is a phrase that repeats itself, and it says it all:

This earth will pass, and with it common trifles,
But God and I will go unendingly.

The apostle Paul said to Philemon, "Greetings to the church in your house." I hope and pray that your marriage will get better and better with each and every passing day, and that the church in your house is a place where the truth of Christ is embraced, where love is expressed, and where God is honored.

6
The Subtle Difference

KEY FOCUS: The way we respond in critical moments can hold the key to success.

Read Matthew 7:24-29.

It is significant to note that sometimes different people can experience the same events and yet be affected by those same events in such radically different ways. For example, two young men have a father who is an alcoholic. One son becomes an alcoholic "because of my father." The other becomes a minister who works with alcoholics "because of my father." Or two people receive the same bad news in the same situation: one is devastated emotionally, coming apart at the seams; the other becomes a tower of strength, an inspiration to everyone she meets.

In Knoxville, Tennessee, some years ago, two

young men were jilted by their intended brides on the same Saturday afternoon. One gave in to self-pity and jumped off the Henley Street Bridge, trying to commit suicide. The other, who was just as broken-hearted, wrote out of his heartache a song that became a popular hit and brought him twenty thousand dollars.

Recently I passed two women I know in a hallway. I greeted them, saying, "My, my, you certainly look nice today." One of them smiled graciously and said, "Thank you." But the other retorted, "Wait a minute; you said I look nice *today*. Does that mean you think I don't *usually* look nice?" Isn't it interesting how the same events, the same situations, and sometimes even the same words can produce such radically different results? Why is this? What makes the difference?

What is the subtle difference that causes different persons to be affected so differently when they are experiencing an identical situation or an identical set of circumstances? The Scriptures are filled with these kinds of happenings. For example, in the Old Testament, we see Moses and Aaron leading the people of Israel out of slavery. The people are scared and frustrated. They squabble and complain. They criticize and gripe and fuss. Moses will not bend to their criticism. Rather, he gives them strong leadership. But Aaron, facing the same kind of criticism, falters and lets them build a golden calf. Why? What was the subtle difference?

In the New Testament, we see it too. Think of the parable of the prodigal son, and how differently the return of the prodigal affected the father and the elder brother. Remember how harshly the prodigal rejected his father and his brother. In effect, he said, "I don't want to be a son, and I don't want to be a brother. I want to be free. I want to be Number One. I don't want to listen to anybody. I want to be in charge!" So, the prodigal takes a portion of the estate and runs off to the far country, where he squanders the money away foolishly and quickly. But then later he comes to his senses, and he returns home in penitence. But look how differently his father and brother are affected by his homecoming. The father is gracious, loving, joyous, forgiving. The elder brother, on the other hand, is grudging, jealous, angry, bitter, and resentful. Why? What is the subtle difference?

Remember Mary and Martha. Jesus comes to their home for dinner. Mary is sensitive to the specialness of the moment. Mary happily sits at the Master's feet and celebrates his presence and drinks in his every word. Meanwhile, Martha gives in to self-pity, feels put upon, and becomes so angry that she explodes out of the kitchen, making an embarrassing scene. Same situation, same day, same place, same events—

but how differently Mary and Martha are affected. Why? What is the subtle difference?

What about Peter and Judas? In the crucial, critical moment each betrayed his Lord, each sold out, each fell short, but Simon Peter bounced back and became one of the courageous leaders of the early church, whereas Judas went out and hanged himself. Why? What was the subtle difference?

Recall Paul and Demas. They were both leaders in the early church's mission to the Gentiles. They were good friends and co-workers. We know about the commitment, the faithfulness, the perseverance, and the impact of the apostle Paul. We know how he was persecuted but never wavered. But look how Demas was affected by the same set of circumstances. We read that haunting verse in the New Testament: "Demas . . . has deserted" (2 Timothy 4:10). Paul stood tall and never wavered, but Demas deserted. Why? What was the subtle difference?

How about Bartimaeus and the rich young ruler? Each of these men had a powerful encounter with Jesus. To each of them, Jesus offered a new hope, a new beginning, a new life. Bartimaeus seized it! He would not be denied this chance. He would not miss this unique opportunity. He threw everything aside—his cloak, his money, his pride—just to get into the presence of Christ. That's all that mattered. He would not be quieted. He knew this was his moment, and he grabbed it. But on the other hand, the rich young ruler turned away sorrowfully. Why? What was the subtle difference?

In all of these instances, what is the subtle difference? Here are three observations.

The Difference Is in the Response

The subtle difference is in how we respond—how we respond to adversity, how we respond to challenge, how we respond to opportunity, how we respond to life. The key is to understand that what happens to us is not nearly as important as how we respond to what happens to us. The key thing is not the circumstances, not the events. The key thing is how we respond!

The poet put it like this:

Two men looked out prison bars;
One saw mud,
The other saw stars.

Notice That the Difference Is Really Not So Subtle

It is dramatic, it is vital, it is crucial—the way you and I respond to things is the single most important fact about our personal lives. It is the difference between defeat and victory; it is the difference between despair and hope; it is the difference between pessimism and optimism; it is the difference between sorrow and joy; it is the difference between death and life.

The Difference We Have Been Talking about Is the Difference Between *Responding* and *Reacting*

There is a big difference between responding and reacting. I'm using here the word *respond* in a positive way, and the word *react* in a negative way. We *react* when we are scared. We *react* when we feel insecure. We *react* when we feel pressed against the wall and we think we have to swell up to giant size to show everybody we can handle the situation.

A *response* is when we give this wonderful miracle we have inside our heads, called a brain, time to compute, time to assess what is happening, and time to figure out what is the appropriate, positive, constructive, creative, Christian thing to do in light of the circumstances. *Responding* (rather than *reacting*) is so important in every dimension of life. It is uniquely crucial in marriage.

Let me illustrate. If a wife says to her husband, "I wish we had more time together," that husband has a choice: he can react or he can respond. The *reaction* could be, "Nag, nag, nag. It's always *something*;

you're always picking on me. I'm doing the best I can." That's a *reaction*. But in the same situation, "I wish we had more time together," the *response* is, "*She* loves *me, she wants to be with me. Isn't it wonderful?* Let's see what we can do about it. Let's find a solution." That's a *response*.

We react out of self-centered personal feelings. We respond out of self-giving concern for others. We react out of littleness; we respond out of bigness.

When I react, I'm thinking of my rights, my position, my place, my feelings, my interests. When I respond, I'm thinking of others, or I'm thinking of a great cause to commit my life to. When I react, I'm thinking of my wants; when I respond, I'm thinking of God's will.

Moses responded; Aaron reacted. The prodigal son's father responded; the elder brother reacted. Mary responded; Martha reacted. Simon Peter responded; Judas reacted. Paul responded; Demas reacted. Bartimaeus responded; the rich young ruler reacted.

General William Booth, who was the founder of the Salvation Army, summed it up graphically some years ago when he said, "Damnation comes from mirrors; salvation comes from windows!" That's just another way of saying destruction, heartache, and misery come from reacting; but life, creativity, and happiness come from responding.

This is a significant key to a happy marriage. The couples who are truly enjoying each other in their marriage today are those who have learned the difference between reacting and responding, and have intentionally chosen to respond rather than react. So, the point is clear: in life, in love, and in marriage, be responders! We have enough reactors in the world. Go out into the world today, and the rest of the days of your life, and be responders.

To paraphrase the great prayer of Saint Francis is to say it all: Lord, make us instruments of your peace. Where there is hatred, let us respond with love; where there is injury, let us respond with pardon; where there is doubt, let us respond with faith; . . . where there is darkness, let us respond with light; where there is sadness, let us respond by bringing joy.

Celebrating the Gift of Marriage

Discussion and Reflection Guide

SALLY D. SHARPE

Note: More questions are provided for each chapter than you may have time to cover in a group setting. If time is a factor, choose those questions that you would like to discuss.

Chapter 1: The Four C's of a Great Marriage

KEY FOCUS: If you want to have a fulfilling marital relationship, you need communication, courtship, commitment, and Christ.

Questions for Reflection and Discussion

1. According to the author, what are the four C's of a great marriage? Do you think any one of these is more important than another? If so, which one, and why?

2. Why is communication so important to any relationship—especially the marriage relationship? What are the four levels of communication in marriage? How can poor communication in any one of these areas affect the others?

3. Read Genesis 1:26-31; Genesis 2:22-25; and Mark 10:6-8. What do these verses tell us about God's design for physical intimacy between husband and wife? Apart from procreation, why did God give husbands and wives the gift of sexual intimacy? In a culture that tends to cheapen and pervert the idea of sex, how can we affirm the sacredness and beauty of God's gift of sex in marriage?

4. Read 1 Corinthians 7:1-5 and Galatians 5:22-23. How can these two passages help husbands and wives to strengthen their relationship in the area of physical intimacy?

5. Besides sexual intimacy, what are some other expressions of physical communication in marriage? What tends to happen when physical touch is limited or lacking in a marriage relationship? How can couples become more intentional about offering physical touch outside the bedroom?

6. How does the author define social communication in marriage? Why is friendship important in the marriage relationship, and how can you

cultivate a friendship with your husband or wife? What are some of the common challenges or obstacles couples face in this area? Brainstorm some practical ways couples can overcome these challenges.

7. The author states that husbands and wives should be not only lovers but also best friends. How would you define what it means for a husband and wife to be "best friends"? How does your answer compare to the author's description of what it means to be best friends?

8. How would you define the term "intellectual communication"? Do you think it is important or necessary for couples to think alike or agree on most issues? Why or why not? What is crucial when it comes to this area of communication in marriage—and why?

9. Why is it important for spouses to communicate about their spiritual lives and cultivate spiritual intimacy? What are some practical ways couples can strengthen their relationship spiritually?

10. Why is courtship just as important after the honeymoon as it is before? Why do you think many couples begin to neglect this area of their relationship after the newlywed phase? What are some practical ways busy couples can keep romance alive?

11. Read Malachi 2:14. As this verse indicates, marriage is a covenant relationship. Look up the word *covenant* in a Bible dictionary. What insights does this definition give you into the marriage covenant? How is a marriage covenant different from a contractual agreement or a trial arrangement? Why is the mind-set of commitment crucial to the covenant of marriage?

12. Do you believe it is possible to "fall out of love"? Why or why not? What should a couple do when the feelings seem to have faded? What are some ways couples can help each other to be committed and remain faithful to their marriage vows?

13. Respond to the following statement: Love is a choice; we must be committed to show love even when we do not feel love. According to Colossians 3:12-14, what does this kind of commitment involve?

14. Read Ecclesiastes 4:9-12. How is Christ "the tie that binds" in the marriage relationship? How can commitment to Christ and his teachings strengthen your relationship with your spouse?

As a Group

As the author observes, one of the unfortunate realities of today's world is the breakdown of family life and the breakup of so many marriages. On a board or chart, list what you believe are some of the causes or contributing factors to this problem. Discuss: *What can we do about this problem as individuals, as families, and as communities of faith?*

At Home

Discuss: *Which of the four C's presents the most difficulties or challenges in our marriage, and why? What can we do to strengthen this area of our relationship?* Be as specific as you can. List your ideas, prioritize them, and then begin working on them one at a time.

Prayer

Dear God, thank you for the gift of marriage. We know that there are many hurting and broken marriages in our world today, yet we rejoice that you are a God of reconciliation and restoration, making all things new. Help us turn to you with yielded and trusting hearts. We acknowledge that we desperately need your help if we are to have a lasting, satisfying, and growing marriage, and we specifically ask for your help in strengthening the four C's of our relationship: communication, courtship, commitment, and most of all, Christ. As we abide in Christ, may we become the husband and wife you call us to be. Amen.

Chapter 2: In Real Estate, It's Location; In Marriage, It's Communication

KEY FOCUS: Couples can benefit from learning some effective techniques for communicating well, including what to avoid.

Questions for Reflection and Discussion

1. What is the author's definition of a "mind game"? Have you ever played mind games with your spouse? Share an example, if you are comfortable doing so. What tends to happen as a result of playing mind games?

2. If it is unrealistic to expect others to read our minds, why do you think many husbands and wives still feel they should not have to ask for something or tell their spouses what they are thinking, wanting, needing, or expecting? Do you feel it is "second rate" to tell your spouse what you want, need, feel, think, and expect? Why or why not?

3. Why is it so important for us to tenderly and lovingly express our expectations and feelings to our spouse? What can help us to do this?

4. Why is it important to use "I" language rather than "you" language? Why does "you" language, especially when accompanied by the

words *always* and *never*, tend to break down communication?

5. How can you and your spouse lovingly encourage each other to use "I" language more often?

6. Why is it inadvisable to discuss emotional issues, complaints, or problems at the family table? When and where are appropriate times and places for these kinds of discussions, and how can you prevent busy schedules from pushing these conversations into inappropriate times and places?

7. How would your marriage and home environment be different if you were to celebrate your love for God and for each other in a spirit of peace, joy, and gratitude whenever you gather around the table? What can you do to make your mealtimes or your other family times together a kind of Holy Communion?

8. Read Genesis 1. According to the Creation story, how did God create the heavens and the earth and all created things? Words have the power to create—as well as to destroy. Have someone else's words ever spoken something into existence in your own life? Share as you are comfortable.

9. Read the following verses: Psalms 59:7; 64:3; 119:103; 140:3; Proverbs 10:20; 12:18; 15:4; 16:24; 20:15. What word pictures are used in these

verses to describe the positive or helpful nature and power of our words? What word pictures are used to describe the negative or hurtful nature and power of our words? Now read Matthew 12:34. What did Jesus say would determine whether we will speak helpful words or hurtful words? What should we do when our words reveal that our hearts are not right with God?

10. Read Ephesians 4:29. Reflect on the following question silently: *Do your words tend to build up or tear down?* How would sharing sincere words of appreciation, love, and encouragement with your spouse on a daily basis affect your relationship? Share some examples of practical ways husbands and wives can build each other up with words.

11. What is "The First Four Minutes" concept? Does your own personal experience validate the observation that the first four minutes of any encounter are extremely significant? Why or why not?

12. How do you and your spouse tend to handle times of "reentry"—those times during your day or evening when you are coming back together after time spent apart? What changes might you need to make? How would your relationship and the atmosphere in your home be different if you spent the first four minutes of reentry into your

relationship loving and affirming each other? This can be difficult when it is dinnertime or when there are children and schedules that cannot be ignored. What are some practical measures you can take to address these challenges?

13. Read John 1:1-5. What do these verses tell us? What did Jesus come to show or reveal about God? What does it mean to say that Jesus is "the measuring stick for communicating"? How can we follow his example as husbands and wives—and as fathers and mothers, brothers and sisters, friends and neighbors?

14. What does it mean to speak in such a way that others see and feel God? What changes might you see in your relationship with your spouse if you were to speak words of life, grace, and love on a daily basis?

As a Group

Have four different couples role-play the following scenarios two times each—first with one spouse sharing his or her expectation in an unloving way, and then with that spouse sharing the same expectation in a tender and loving way:

One spouse expects the other to complete a household chore.

One spouse expects to be greeted with a kiss.
One spouse wants to go out for dinner at the end of a busy day.
One spouse needs some quiet time alone to work on a project.

Discuss: *What kind of reaction or response was generated by each approach? How can husbands and wives encourage and help each other express their needs, wants, thoughts, and feelings in a tender and loving way?*

At Home

Practice "The First Four Minutes" concept each day this week. Every time you reenter the relationship after being apart, affirm each other with words and physical demonstrations of love and affection. Resolve to give each other your time, attention, and love for four minutes before discussing any problems, issues, or needs. Discuss in advance any challenges or obstacles you may face and how you will address them. Throughout the week, observe how this time affects the atmosphere of your relationship and your home.

Prayer

Loving God, you demonstrated the importance of communication by sending your own Son into the world both to show and to tell us what you are like, how much you love us, and how we are to live. May we follow Christ's example in all of our relationships, especially the relationship of husband and wife. Help us speak words of life, love, and grace to each other every day, building each other up rather than tearing each other down. Remind us that our words have great power, and help us choose them wisely and speak them lovingly. May we minister to each other with our words, and may our marriage be blessed and strengthened as a result. We ask these things in Jesus' name. Amen.

Chapter 3: Celebrating the Gift of Marriage

KEY FOCUS: If you want to have a joyful, celebrative marriage, don't be crabby, critical, or controlling.

Questions for Reflection and Discussion

1. Respond to the following statement: In most cases, couples can make marriage work—and the key word is *work*. What does it mean to say that marriage takes "work"? Why do you think so many couples today are either unwilling or unable to "make marriage work"?

2. How would you describe someone who is "crabby"? What are some common causes of crabbiness? Discuss how each of the following can help alleviate crabbiness and restore one's joy:
   • an awareness of God's unfailing love, mercy, and grace
   • a sense of gratitude or thankfulness
   • a sense of humor
   • other(s)

3. How is the marriage relationship affected if one spouse is often grumpy or crabby? Why is it wrong for husbands and wives to expect their spouse to accept and/or excuse their crabby attitudes? Read Colossians 3:12-13. According to

these verses, how are we to treat others—*including our spouses?*

4. What is criticism, and what does it mean to criticize someone? How are we judging others when we criticize them?

5. Read Matthew 7:1-5 and Romans 14:10-13. According to these verses, what happens when we judge or criticize others, and why should we not do this? Now read Romans 3:23 and John 8:7. According to these verses, who is qualified to judge others?

6. Why is criticism especially destructive in marriage? How is *constructive* criticism different? Do you believe this kind of criticism is ever acceptable or advisable in marriage? Explain your answer.

7. What is an *encourager*? Using the language of Ephesians 4:29, what does it mean to encourage others? How can husbands and wives encourage each other in this way?

8. A common cause of conflict in marriage is the struggle for control—the desire to have it "my way." What kind of messages does the "I want it my way" attitude communicate? What fears or insecurities might be behind this need for power or control? Read Luke 9:23. According to this verse, who is to lead or be in charge of our lives? How does surrendering our lives to Christ—

daily denying ourselves and following him—enable us to relinquish the need to have our way with our spouse, as well as with others?

9. How can ongoing courtship be a practical way to eliminate "power struggles" in marriage? What kinds of things might this involve?

10. What impact might it have upon your marriage if you were to begin each morning with this thought: *How can I bring joy and happiness and pleasure and support to this life-mate of mine whom I love so much?* What can enable you to do this?

11. Sometimes we find ourselves in a situation where we can choose either to make ourselves look good or to make our mate look good. Why do we sometimes find the latter choice so difficult? Read Romans 12:3, 10; James 4:10; and 1 Peter 5:10. What instruction and encouragement do we find in these verses?

12. Read John 13:34-35. What does it mean to love others the way that Christ has loved us? How would you describe this kind of love? Share some practical ways you can love your spouse in this way each and every day. (See the following "As a Group" activity.)

As a Group

On a board or chart, make a list of things Jesus did to demonstrate love. Refer to the Gospels to make your list as exhaustive as possible. Beside each of these words or phrases, write one or more specific, practical ways that a husband and wife might offer a similar expression of love for each other. Be as realistic and practical in the examples you choose as you can.

At Home

Discuss together: *What was our relationship like during our courtship, engagement, and early days of marriage? What activities, practices, or habits of those days that may have "fallen away" do we want or need to resume? How can we cultivate a sense of "courtship" in our relationship?* Make a list of specific things you can do individually and together, and make a plan for putting these things into practice.

Prayer

Lord, marriage is truly a beautiful gift, yet so often we ruin and destroy this precious gift with our negative attitudes and behaviors. Today we ask you to open our hearts and minds so that we may come to recognize the ways we may be poisoning our own marriages. Help us replace destructive habits such as crabbiness, criticism, and the need to control with life-giving prac-

tices such as gratitude, respect, and grace. Enable us through the power of your Holy Spirit to love our mate in the same way that you love us, following the example of your Son, Jesus Christ. It is in his name that we pray. Amen.

Chapter 4: Happy Marriage: It's All about Choices

KEY FOCUS: In living and in marriage, often our choices control our outcomes.

Questions for Reflection and Discussion

1. Why do you think we often allow our emotions to determine how we respond to others, rather than choosing by an act of the will how we will respond? Discuss the following statement: Regardless of your circumstances and emotions, in every moment you have the opportunity to choose whether you will build up or tear down your spouse.

2. Read Matthew 5:9. In *John Wesley's Notes on the Bible*, Wesley writes that peacemakers are those who "out of love to God and man, do all possible good to all possible men." What would it mean for you to "do all possible good" to your spouse? How might this help to foster peace in your relationship?

3. Read Psalm 39:1 and James 1:26. According to these verses, what is the key to being a peacemaker and an encourager rather than a troublemaker and a discourager? What does it mean to "bridle the tongue"? How can we do this?

4. Why do you think some husbands and wives think it is their duty and right to point out all the negative qualities and habits of their mate? Why is this such a destructive habit? How can couples help each other break this habit?

5. Why do you think some people choose to focus on the negative rather than the positive? How do you feel when you're around someone like this?

6. Who are the encouragers in your life—those who focus on the positive and build you up?

7. Review the three discoveries or observations that Laura Huxley shares in her book *You're Not the Target*. Think of a time when you encouraged or built up your spouse. How did it make you feel? Now think of a time when you discouraged or tore down your spouse. How did you feel afterward? Would you agree that making others feel better also makes *you* feel better? Why or why not?

8. If making others feel better is much more rewarding than making them feel worse, why do you think some people still choose to tear others down with their words? What might this reveal about their own need(s)? How might you encourage or minister to such a person—perhaps even your own spouse?

9. Often we think of encouragement as merely kind words. What other things can we do to

offer encouragement to others? Which of these things do you need to be more intentional in doing for your spouse?

10. Read Proverbs 17:22. In what ways is laughter like good medicine? Why is laughter so important to a healthy, happy marriage?

11. What is the difference between laughing *with* your spouse and laughing at your spouse? How can couples use laughter appropriately to help diffuse tense or angry moments? Share a specific example from your own marriage, if you are comfortable doing so.

12. What are some ways we "punish" our spouses when they anger, frustrate, or disappoint us? How do these tactics only make things worse? Do you tend to be more prone to punish or to pardon, and why do you think this is so?

13. Read Matthew 6:14-15. According to these verses, why is it important to forgive others? Do you think our inclination to forgive or pardon others is determined by the measure of our appreciation for God's forgiveness or pardon of us? Why or why not?

As a Group

Peacemakers work for peace in two ways: (1) they promote or keep peace before it is broken, and

(2) they recover it once it has been broken. Break into two groups. Have one group brainstorm ways that couples can promote peace in their relationship and at home *before* peace is broken; have the other group brainstorm ways couples can recover or restore peace *after* it has been broken. Come back together and share ideas.

At Home

Discuss: *How can we increase the laughter in our relationship and our home?* Each day this week, try to share with your spouse a funny story, a good joke, or a humorous incident from your day. Watch a comedy and enjoy laughing together. Agree to "lighten up" and allow laughter to defuse tense moments. Remember not to use sarcasm, teasing, or any other kind of humor that might hurt each other's feelings. Talk about the kinds of humor that might be hurtful, and agree to avoid them.

Prayer

O God, you call us to be peacemakers, for you are a God of peace. The Scriptures tell us that you are our peace; and we know from experience that there is no real peace apart from you. Yet often we turn from you and your ways, choosing to speak and to act harshly toward each other. Forgive us,

Lord. Help us to love as Jesus loved, always building up rather than tearing down. And when we fail, help us to be quick to forgive each other, just as you always forgive us. May your peace and joy fill our hearts so that they spill over, splashing generously onto each other and everyone we meet. In Jesus' name we pray. Amen.

Chapter 5: The Church in Your House

KEY FOCUS: The Christian home should be where love of God and love of others is first expressed and lived out.

Questions for Reflection and Discussion

1. How can a negative attitude—on the part of one spouse or both spouses—wreak havoc in a marriage? What are some possible outcomes or consequences of a negative attitude in the marriage relationship? How can couples prevent a negative attitude from leading to anger, bitterness, resentment, and hostility?

2. Read Philemon 1-7. In his letter to Philemon, Paul sends greetings "to the church in your house" (verse 2). In what ways should every Christian home be a "house church"? What can you and your spouse do to make your home a "house church"?

3. Read John 8:32. How, or in what ways, does the truth set us free?

4. Read John 14:17, John 16:13, and John 17:16-18. Then discuss the following questions: With all the conflicting ideas bombarding us today and vying for our allegiance, how can we know the truth? How can we discern truth from deception, propaganda, and outright lies?

5. Read John 1:1. According to the author, what is the meaning of the Greek word *logos* used for "Word" in this verse? What does this tell us about Jesus?

6. What does it mean to say that Jesus Christ is our measuring stick for truth? How can we measure everything we see, read, and hear by the standard of truth we see in Jesus Christ?

7. What does it mean to build a marriage on truth? Practically speaking, how can couples embrace and live out the truth of Christ in their relationship and in their home? What might this look like on an everyday basis?

8. Read John 14:8-10 and 1 John 4:8. What do these verses tell us about God and Jesus? What one word characterizes both Father and Son?

9. Read 1 John 4:7-21. What do these verses say is the reason we are to love one another, and how is this possible?

10. According to 1 John 4:12, what happens when we love one another? According to verses 16 and 17, what happens when God lives in us and we live in love? If love were "made complete" or "perfected" between a husband and wife, what do you think their marriage would be like?

11. Read 1 Corinthians 10:31. In this verse, the Greek word for "glory" means honor, praise, and worship. What does it mean to do all for the glory—

or honor—of God? How can you bring glory and honor to God through your marriage?

12. Why is Phillips Brooks's philosophy—"Commit your life to God, believe in him, lean on him, and in the last analysis nothing will ever overcome you"—also a good "prescription" for a satisfying, lasting marriage?

As a Group

The author writes, "We must get back to emphasizing and cultivating Christian marriage and the Christian home." Work together to compose definitions or descriptions of the terms "Christian marriage" and "Christian home." Write the definitions on a board or chart. Below the definitions, list specific ways that couples can strive to live out the kind of marriage you have described. Discuss: *In addition to these things, what else can couples do to cultivate a Christian home?* Add the group's ideas to the list. Ask: *Of all these ideas we've listed, which do you think pose the most challenges for couples today, and why?*

At Home

Agree to prayerfully consider the following questions for several days:

- Is our home a place where the truth of Christ is embraced?
- Is our home a place where love is expressed?
- Is our home a place where God is honored?

Set a time and place to share your thoughts with each other and discuss how your home might become an even stronger "house church."

Prayer

Dear God, we praise and thank you for expressing your great love for us through your Son, Jesus Christ. Because he came into the world and lived among us, we have a clear picture of what you are like and how you want us to live. Help us model our individual lives, our marriages, and our homes after his example of perfect love. May we always look to him as our "measuring stick for truth," evaluating everything we see and hear by the standard of truth we see in him. Our desire is to keep you in the center of our lives, so that all we do may honor and glorify you. Help us to have marriages and homes where the truth of Christ is embraced, the love of Christ is expressed, and the name of Christ is honored. Amen.

Chapter 6: The Subtle Difference

KEY FOCUS: The way we respond in critical moments can hold the key to success.

Questions for Reflection and Discussion

1. The author shares several examples of people who experienced the same or similar events and yet were affected by those events in radically different ways. In each example, what is the obvious difference between the two outcomes or results? What do you think might account for such different responses to identical or similar circumstances?

2. Read Exodus 17:1-7. How did Moses respond to the people's complaints? What happened as a result? Now read Exodus 32:1-4. How did Aaron respond to the people's complaints and demands? According to Exodus 32:30-35, what happened as a result? Reread Exodus 17:4. What did Moses do that Aaron did not do?

3. In your own words, explain why our response is so much more important than our circumstances. Share an example from your own life or from the life of someone you know to illustrate how the right response can turn defeat into victory, despair into hope, or sadness into joy.

4. What tends to happen when we focus on our circumstances? Read Psalm 121:1-2. According to these verses, where should our focus be? What is God called in these verses? How can we know that God is able to help us, regardless of the magnitude or complexity of our situation, problem, or need?

5. The hymn "Turn Your Eyes Upon Jesus," written by Helen H. Lemmel in 1922, includes this refrain:

   Turn your eyes upon Jesus

   . . . .
   And the things of earth will grow strangely dim

   According to this hymn, what happens when we keep our focus on Jesus rather than on our circumstances? Have you found this to be true in your own life? Practically speaking, what can help us to keep our focus on Jesus in the middle of painful, difficult, or challenging circumstances?

6. Read Romans 8:28. How can this verse give us hope in the midst of difficult, challenging, or changing circumstances? There are two "parts" of this promise. What is God's part or responsibility? What is our part or responsibility?

7. What is the difference between responding and reacting? Discuss the difference in our thoughts and concerns when we respond as opposed to when we react.
8. Why is choosing to respond rather than react vitally important in marriage?
9. How can choosing to respond rather than react help prevent arguments and promote peace?
10. Read 1 Corinthians 2:16 and Romans 12:2. Why is it vitally important for us to have the mind of Christ and renew our minds if we are to be responders rather than reactors? How do we do this?

As a Group

Divide into small groups. Assign each group two or three of the following Scriptures:

Psalm 33:20
Psalm 46:10
Psalm 121:1-2
Proverbs 15:1
Isaiah 26:3
Matthew 7:12
John 14:1
Romans 8:28
Romans 12:2-3

Romans 12:10
Philippians 4:8
Colossians 3:13

Give the following instructions:
(1) Read your assigned Scriptures and identify the insights or principles they contain that can help us to be responders rather than reactors.
(2) Discuss practical ways couples can apply this wisdom on a daily basis.

Come back together as a full group to share and discuss ideas.

At Home

Take a few moments to reflect silently on the following questions: *Do you tend to see the glass as half full or half empty? Why? Do you tend to respond or to react? What about your spouse?* Share your thoughts with each other—with sensitivity and love. Discuss: *How can we encourage and help each other to respond rather than react? When one of us reacts, how can we "defuse" the situation and keep from perpetuating a cycle of reactions?*

Prayer

Print the prayer of Saint Francis of Assisi on a board or chart, and close by having participants say the prayer in unison:

Lord, make me an instrument of Thy peace;
where there is hatred, let me sow love;
where there is injury, pardon;
where there is doubt, faith;
where there is despair, hope;
where there is darkness, light;
and where there is sadness, joy.
O Divine Master,
grant that I may not so much seek to be consoled as to
*   console;*
to be understood, as to understand;
to be loved, as to love;
for it is in giving that we receive,
it is in pardoning that we are pardoned,
and it is in dying that we are born to Eternal Life.
Amen.